BE A WASTE WARRIOR

T0012346

FOOD WARRIOR

GOING GREEN

by Claudia Martin

Consultant: David Hawksett, BSc

BEARPORT
PUBLISHING

Minneapolis, Minnesota

Credits: cover, © Gary Perkin/Shutterstock; 1, © Monkey Business Images/Shutterstock; 4l, © Michael Zysman/Shutterstock; 4–5b, © Simon Kadula/Shutterstock; 5t, © I viewfinder/Shutterstock; 6t, © Kamonchai/Shutterstock; 6b, © GUNDAM_Ai/Shutterstock; 7, © Pixavril/Shutterstock; 8b, © Rudy Umans/Shutterstock; 9, © Manoej Paateel/Shutterstock; 10–11b, © Tim UR/Shutterstock; 11t, © Rblfmr/Shutterstock; 12, © Avigator Fortuner/Shutterstock; 13, © Jeeranan Thongpan/Shutterstock; 14–15b, © Lorenzo Gambaro/Shutterstock; 15t, © Daisy Daisy/Shutterstock; 16–17b, © Maxim Blinkov/Shutterstock; 17r, © Mattjamesphotography/Shutterstock; 18, © YoloStock/Shutterstock; 19, © Kurhan/Shutterstock; 20, © Ryosha/Shutterstock; 21, © VaLiza/Shutterstock; 22, © Luciano Joaquim/Shutterstock; 23t, © 22August/Shutterstock; 23b, © Switlana Sonyashna/Shutterstock; 24–25b, © Suteelak Phundang/Shutterstock; 25t, © Yalcin Sonat/Shutterstock; 26, © Olena Yakobchuk/Shutterstock; 27, © Garetsworkshop/Shutterstock.

Editor: Sarah Eason
Proofreader: Jennifer Sanderson
Designer: Paul Myerscough
Illustrator: Jessica Moon
Picture Researcher: Rachel Blount

Library of Congress Cataloging-in-Publication Data

Names: Martin, Claudia, author.
Title: Food warrior : going green / by Claudia Martin.
Description: Minneapolis, Minnesota : Bearport Publishing Company, [2021] |
    Series: Be a waste warrior! | Includes bibliographical references and
    index.
Identifiers: LCCN 2020030874 (print) | LCCN 2020030875 (ebook) | ISBN
    9781647476977 (library binding) | ISBN 9781647477042 (paperback) | ISBN
    9781647477110 (ebook)
Subjects: LCSH: Food waste—Juvenile literature. | Refuse and refuse
    disposal—Environmental aspects—Juvenile literature.
Classification: LCC TD804 .M27 2021 (print) | LCC TD804 (ebook) | DDC
    363.72/856—dc23
LC record available at https://lccn.loc.gov/2020030874
LC ebook record available at https://lccn.loc.gov/2020030875

For more information, write to Bearport Publishing, 5357 Penn Avenue South, Minneapolis, MN 55419. Printed in the United States of America.

CONTENTS

THE BATTLE TO SAVE EARTH!

Have you ever tossed your leftover salad in the trash? Or been shocked by how many cans, bottles, and wrappers your family goes through? You're not the only one! Wasted food and tossed packaging are a big part of global **pollution**. But you can do your part in the fight against waste. It's easier than you think to become a waste warrior.

The Three Problems with Waste

Heaps of Garbage Most of our household garbage is thrown into **landfills**. But when waste breaks down in landfills, it can harm our environment. **Plastic** can leak harmful things into the soil and air. Waste in landfills lets off methane gas as it breaks down. On top of that, the waste in landfills just sits there—stored for a future generation to deal with. That is why waste warriors avoid creating waste!

Our waste piles up in landfills.

Wasted Resources

Sometimes, we put too much pasta on our plate and have to toss the extra. We might leave fruit on the counter, and it starts to get moldy. Then we have to buy more food to replace the food we didn't even eat. But growing food uses our planet's limited **natural resources**.

Fossil fuels are burned to power this canning factory.

Polluted Planet
We create pollution when we burn **fossil fuels**, such as **coal** and **oil**, to power the factories that put beans in cans or make bags to hold our chips. Then, we burn more fossil fuels as we transport our food by truck or airplane around the world. When fossil fuels are burned, they release **carbon dioxide** and other gases that trap the sun's heat around Earth. This causes temperatures to rise, and these hotter temperatures affect the planet, creating global **climate change**.

When we throw away pizza, we are trashing tomatoes that used water to grow.

The Six Rs

Want to become a food waste warrior? Here are six tools you can use in the battle against waste. But you don't need to manage every one of them all the time. Every effort, no matter how small, takes us in the right direction!

Refuse If you have a choice, say "No, thank you!" to plastic bags and unneeded packaging when you're buying food or drinks.

You can help in the battle against food waste by refusing plastic straws.

Reduce Try to put less food in the trash by buying only what you need.

Reuse Before throwing out food scraps, ask an adult if they could be used for something else—such as a tasty soup.

Repair Ask an adult for help fixing old, torn bags. Then, you can use them to carry food home from the store.

Recycle Try to **recycle** all the metal, glass, plastic, and paper packaging you can, so it can be made into something new.

Rot Compost unwanted plant-based foods so they can rot away.

Always reuse or recycle plastic packaging.

A compost bin helps your food rot away.

Eat Up

Apples turning brown in the fruit bowl? Carrots looking lonely at the back of the fridge? It can happen to the best of us! But when our food goes bad before we've even taken a bite, it wastes all the natural resources that went into making it, too. Just think about water!

The plants we eat need water to grow. Animals that give us meat, milk, and eggs need water to drink. And it all adds up! On average, farming takes up 70 percent of the fresh water used globally every year. Yet more than one-quarter of the world's population—two billion people—do not have access to safe drinking water. We definitely shouldn't waste it on food we don't eat! How can a waste warrior help? Before you eat those crackers, check out that lonely carrot in your fridge!

Growing our plant crops uses up a huge amount of water. These crops are being sprayed with water.

What a Waste!

About 1,320 gallons (5,000 L) of water are used to produce the food an average American eats in just one day.

Finding clean water to drink can be a daily battle for many people.

Ready to reduce food waste? The first thing to do is check **expiration** dates for food. Canned and dried foods can last a long time, sometimes years, before they expire. But fresh plant and animal foods go bad much faster. When you're hungry for a snack, choose the food with the approaching expiration date. If you notice something is about to go bad, try some creative ways to use those foods fast.

Warriors Can Try:

Try out these fun ways to use soon-to-expire food. Find a simple recipe, then ask an adult to help you cook.

- Cook softened fruit in a little juice and add a cobbler topping.

- Use leftover onion, carrot tops, wilted celery, and other vegetable scraps to make soup.

- Blend together soon-to-expire milk and fruit for a tasty smoothie.

- Mix uneaten meat, fish, veggies, or cheese with lettuce for a healthy salad.

BEST BY

Even the leaves
of vegetables can
be made into soup!

Check your fridge
regularly to make
sure you use food
before it goes bad.

COMPOST YOUR WASTE

Food can rot into **nutrients** that plants use to grow. It's nature's way of recycling! So what's the harm if we toss food into a landfill? The answer might surprise you.

If an apple core is left next to the tree it fell out of, it will rot in a process called **biodegrading**. But when the same apple is put in a landfill, it is squashed tightly next to a lot of other waste. In this almost-airless environment, methane gas forms as the waste breaks down. If a landfill releases methane gas, the gas traps heat around Earth, causing climate change. Luckily, when waste warriors rot food in a large, airy compost bin, the air stops methane from being released. Problem solved!

Some modern landfills trap methane, but others do not.

You can see biodegrading in action with these strawberries!

What a Waste!

Every year, more than 30 million tons (27 million MT) of wasted food makes its way into U.S. landfills.

Starting a compost bin is a great way to reduce food waste. Plus (bonus!) you can use the resulting compost to help grow your own delicious fruits and vegetables.

To start composting, you will need a bin with a lid. If you have outside space, you could use a really large bin, up to 3 feet (1 m) across, but a little bin under the kitchen counter is good for collecting compost inside. Just add your fruit and vegetable scraps, egg shells, and bread crusts. After a few months, your waste will have turned to mushy soil—your compost is ready! Ask an adult to help you learn more about composting and get started.

Warriors Can Try:

When making your planet-saving compost, remember to stay away from these items.

- Dairy **products**, such as cheese and yogurt
- Meat and meat bones
- Fish
- Fats and oils

Try keeping
a compost pail
in your kitchen
for food scraps.

Once your compost waste
has fully broken down,
you can use it to feed
plants. Way to go,
Waste Warrior!

TAKE YOUR OWN BAGS

Plastic bags are everywhere! They are ready to be stuffed with groceries after we check out. We use them to collect fruits and vegetables. There might even be bags in the meat section at your store. And all these plastic bags add up.

Plastic can take up to 1,000 years to break down, depending on the type of plastic. The problem is that the **bacteria** that break down our food do not easily eat plastic. What's even worse? As plastic slowly breaks down, harmful chemicals can be released. These chemicals may stop our bodies from working properly. You can help make a positive change by remembering to take your own bags to the store.

Plastic waste dumped on beaches makes its way into our oceans and then back up onto our beaches again.

What a Waste!

In the United States, we use around 100 billion plastic shopping bags a year, but only 10 percent of them are recycled, because they are not usually accepted in curbside recycling bins.

Plastic waste can be deadly for ocean animals. This porcupinefish is trapped in a plastic bag.

An excellent way for a waste warrior to reduce plastic bag waste is to refuse! Politely say no to plastic bags at the store. Instead, bring your own reusable bags to carry your food. When you get home, empty the bags and wash them if they are dirty. Then, put them by the front door or in the trunk of the car so you'll have them ready for the next shopping trip.

Warriors Can Try:

Try these alternatives to using plastic bags.

- Buy long-lasting shopping bags made from cloth or recycled plastic.

- Sew your own bags from old T-shirts or ripped sheets.

- Ask your local store if you can use reusable containers when shopping from bulk bins.

- Leave fruits and vegetables loose in your cart or bundle them in reusable bags.

Try shopping with a string bag—it's a great way to carry fruits and vegetables home.

Shopping for food that is sold unpackaged can help reduce waste.

SAY NO TO STRAWS

Plastic straws can give you a quick sip. But after you're done with your drink, what happens? Plastic straws are not usually recycled or reused, so they end up as waste in the trash.

Although plastic straws are often made from a recyclable type of plastic called polypropylene, straws cannot usually be recycled at recycling plants because they are too small and light. When plastic items arrive at a recycling plant, they are sent down conveyer belts and sorted into different kinds of materials. However, light objects, such as plastic straws, usually fall between the cracks on the conveyor belts. These items that drop off the line at a recycling plant often end up in a landfill or—even worse—floating in the ocean. Every year, millions of straws end up in bodies of water, where they may be swallowed by animals from turtles to seals and fish. The answer for a waste warrior: don't use straws!

Plastic straws can easily fall between the cracks of conveyor belts.

Serious waste warriors say no to plastic straws!

What a Waste!

It is estimated that 500 million plastic straws are used every single day in the United States.

To reduce waste, simply say no thanks when you're offered a straw with your drink. You can also skip a plastic lid for your cup. Then, you can sip your drink the old-fashioned way and reduce plastic waste while you're doing it! If you really like the fun of a straw, think about getting your own reusable straw that you can bring around with you.

Warriors Can Try:

If your favorite restaurant or cafe is still handing out plastic straws, try writing to them.

- Explain why plastic straws can be such a big problem.

- Include some facts and figures about straw waste.

- Give examples of amazing animals that are harmed by straw waste.

- Ask an adult for help sending your note.

If you love to sip with a straw, get a reusable glass or metal straw to clean and use over and over!

Straws made from bamboo are a better alternative to plastic straws.

AVOID PROBLEM PACKAGING

The grocery store is full of things we can't eat. It's true! Take a look around and you'll see glass, metal, cardboard, and plastic. Why are we buying all of this? Often, we don't have a choice. Our food is wrapped up in packaging. But not all food packaging is treated the same! Some items can be recycled, but others are made of mixed materials and can't be recycled.

At a recycling plant, items made from glass, metal, cardboard, paper, and plastic are separated by the material they're made from. Then, they can be melted or treated and reshaped into new products, including new food packaging. However, when packaging is made from different materials that are stuck to each other, it is very difficult to make into something new. Instead, these items usually end up in a landfill. Be on the lookout for mixed-material monsters. Waste warriors are wise recyclers!

When plastic is recycled, it is often broken down into a lot of tiny pieces that can then be reshaped into new items.

Potato chip bags are often made with layers of metal and plastic, so they can't be recycled.

What a Waste!

It takes only a few minutes to eat a bag of potato chips but the empty bag could take as long as 80 years to break down.

Being able to spot mixed materials is a big first step on the road to recycling responsibly. When you're buying food in a store, try to choose items packaged in just one material, such as a glass bottle of juice rather than a carton made from both plastics and paper. Some mixed-material packaging, such as glass bottles with metal caps, can be separated at home, before putting the different parts in curbside recycling bins. Remember, waste warriors recycle whatever they can!

Warriors Can Try:

Here are some types of packaging that commonly use mixed materials.

- Paper containers used to hold drinks and sauces often have a plastic lining to stop them from leaking.

- Cardboard tubes used for some chips and cookies often have metal lining to keep food fresh.

- Shiny bags used to hold chips are made of foil and plastic to keep them lightweight and strong.

Try to buy food item wrapped in just one type of packaging.

When waste warriors choose eco-friendly groceries, producers make more of them—and fewer products that are harmful to the environment.

Eco-Activity
Make Juice Carton Seed Starters

Growing your own fruits and vegetables is a great way to cut down on food packaging waste. It's also a great way to reduce fuel used when food is transported between farms and supermarkets across the country—or even around the world. By using **upcycled** plastic juice cartons to grow your seeds, you're also helping to solve yet another waste problem as you reuse!

You will need:
- Scissors
- Empty plastic juice cartons
- Materials for decorating your cartons
- Soil
- Seeds suitable for planting at your home

1 Using scissors, carefully cut the top off your plastic juice cartons.

2 Choose how to decorate your cartons. Try to pick eco-friendly materials.

3 Decorate your seed starter planter base.

4 Next, fill most of the planter with soil.

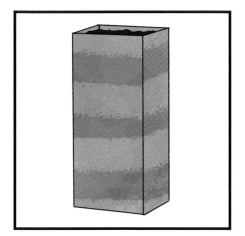

5 Following the instructions on the seed packet, plant seeds in your planter.

6 Leave the planter on a warm windowsill, watering a little when the soil looks dry.

7 If your seedlings begin to outgrow their starter box, transfer them to larger pots.

8 Watch your plants grow until you have a tasty meal of home-grown fruits or veggies.

Glossary

bacteria tiny, very simple living things

biodegrading the breaking down of waste by living things, such as bacteria and fungi

carbon dioxide an invisible gas in the air that is released when coal and oil are burned

climate change the change in climate and weather patterns, including the warming of Earth's air and oceans, due to human activity and natural events

coal a solid fuel that is found in the ground and is made from the remains of animals and plants that lived long ago

compost rotted food and other natural materials that can be used to feed soil

expiration the end of the time during which a food is eatable

fossil fuels fuels made from the remains of animals and plants that lived long ago

landfills pits where waste is dumped and then covered by soil

natural resources useful materials found in nature, such as plants, water, metals, and coal

nutrients natural materials, such as nitrogen or phosphorus, that help plants grow

oil also called petroleum; a liquid fuel that is found in the ground and made from the remains of dead animals and plants

plastic a machine-made material, usually made from oil, that can be shaped when soft, then sets to be hard or flexible

pollution any harmful material that is put into the ground, air, or water

products things that are made then offered for sale

recycle to collect, sort, and treat waste so it is turned into materials that can be used again

upcycled to have turned old materials or products into new items

Read More

Archer, Joe and Caroline Craig. *Plant, Cook, Eat! A Children's Cookbook.* Watertown, MA: Charlesbridge, 2018.

Enz, Tammy. *Incredible Snack Package Science (Edge Books. Recycled Science).* North Mankato, MN: Capstone Press, 2017.

Mangor, Jodie. *Climate Change and Food Production (Taking Earth's Temperature).* Vero Beach, FL: Rourke Educational Media, 2019.

O'Brien, Cynthia. *The Impact of Food and Farming (Impact on Earth).* New York: Crabtree Publishing Company, 2020.

Learn More Online

1. Go to **www.factsurfer.com**
2. Enter "**Food Warrior**" into the search box.
3. Click on the cover of this book to see a list of websites.

Index